PANAMA
FACTS AND TRIVIA

WILL EASTON

Copyright © 2025 Will Easton

All rights reserved.

CONTENTS

INTRODUCTION TO PANAMA 1
PEOPLE AND CULTURE 4
PANAMA'S POLITICAL HISTORY 7
PANAMA CANAL: THE HEART OF THE NATION 11
ECONOMY AND INDUSTRY 15
PANAMA'S CUISINE 19
TOURISM AND TRAVEL IN PANAMA 23
WILDLIFE AND BIODIVERSITY 28
PANAMA TODAY AND TOMORROW 32

INTRODUCTION TO PANAMA

- Geographical Location: Panama is located in Central America, bordered by Costa Rica to the west, Colombia to the east, the Pacific Ocean to the south, and the Caribbean Sea to the north.

- Capital City: The capital of Panama is Panama City, which is also the largest city in the country.

- Panama's Area: The country covers an area of about 75,000 square miles (195,000 km²), making it one of the smallest countries in Central America.

- Population: As of 2024, Panama has a population of approximately 4.5 million people.

- Climate: Panama has a tropical climate, with a wet season from May to November and a dry season from December to April. The country's location near the equator gives it warm temperatures year-round.

PANAMA FACTS AND TRIVIA

- Panama Canal: The Panama Canal is one of the most important artificial waterways in the world, connecting the Atlantic and Pacific Oceans. It plays a crucial role in global trade and has shaped the country's history and economy.

- Independence: Panama declared its independence from Colombia on November 3, 1903, after years of political instability. It became a sovereign nation with the help of the United States.

- Official Language: The official language of Panama is Spanish. However, English is widely spoken, especially in the business and tourist sectors.

- Currency: The official currency is the Balboa (PAB), although the U.S. dollar (USD) is also widely accepted and used as the main currency in daily transactions.

- Time Zone: Panama is in the Eastern Standard Time (EST) zone, and the country does not observe daylight saving time.

- Panama's Flag: The flag of Panama consists of two equal horizontal bands of white with a red star in the top-left corner and a blue star in the bottom-right corner. The red and blue stars symbolize the country's political parties, and the white represents peace.

- Panama's Diversity: Panama is a culturally diverse nation, with influences from Indigenous peoples, Afro-descendants, Spanish settlers, and immigrants from various parts of the world, particularly from China, the Caribbean, and Europe.

- Panama's Economy: The country has one of the most stable economies in Latin America, driven by services, banking, tourism, and trade facilitated by the Panama Canal.

- **Biodiversity**: Panama is home to rich biodiversity, including a variety of flora and fauna. It is often considered one of the most biodiverse countries in the world, with numerous species of birds, insects, mammals, and plants.

PEOPLE AND CULTURE

- Ethnic Diversity: Panama is a melting pot of cultures, with people of various ethnic backgrounds, including mestizo (mixed Indigenous and European ancestry), Afro-Panamanian, Indigenous, European, Chinese, and Middle Eastern descent.

- Languages Spoken: While Spanish is the official language, there are several Indigenous languages spoken, such as Ngäbere, Buglere, and Kuna. English is also widely spoken, particularly in business and among the expatriate community.

- Indigenous Groups: Panama is home to several Indigenous groups, including the Guna (or Kuna), Emberá, Ngäbe-Buglé, and Wounaan. These groups maintain their unique cultural traditions, languages, and ways of life.

- Afro-Panamanian Heritage: A significant portion of Panama's population is of African descent, primarily descendants of enslaved Africans brought during the colonial period. Afro-Panamanian culture is rich in music, dance, and culinary traditions.

- **Religion**: The majority of Panamanians are Roman Catholic (around 70%), with a significant Protestant minority (about 15%). There is also a growing community of Evangelicals and small groups of Jewish, Muslim, and Indigenous spiritual communities.

- **Music and Dance**: Panama has a vibrant music scene, with genres such as salsa, reggae en español, cumbia, and panamanian folk music like tipico and tamborito. The Panamanian tamborito is a traditional dance that features colorful costumes and lively drumming.

- **Carnival**: Carnival is one of the most celebrated events in Panama. It takes place before Lent and involves parades, dancing, music, and vibrant costumes, especially in Panama City and Las Tablas. The carnival in Las Tablas is particularly famous for its large-scale celebrations.

- **Cultural Festivals**: Panama hosts numerous festivals throughout the year, celebrating its diverse culture. Notable festivals include the Festival de la Mejorana (traditional music), the Festival de Diablos y Congos (celebrating Afro-Panamanian culture), and Semana Santa (Holy Week).

- **Panamanian Cuisine**: Panamanian food is a mix of Indigenous, Afro, and Spanish influences. Some popular dishes include sancocho (chicken soup with vegetables), arroz con pollo (rice with chicken), empanadas (fried turnovers), tamales, and ceviche (marinated seafood).

- **Traditional Clothing**: The traditional pollera, a colorful dress, is worn by women during cultural celebrations and festivals. Men often wear guayaberas, lightweight shirts suitable for the tropical climate.

- **Family Structure**: Family is an essential part of Panamanian life. Extended families often live close to each other, and gatherings are common. Respect for elders and strong community ties are significant aspects of the culture.

- Panamanian Art: Panama has a growing art scene, with a blend of traditional and modern influences. Mola is an iconic form of Indigenous art made by the Guna people, characterized by bright designs sewn into fabric.

- Sports: Baseball is the most popular sport in Panama, with the country producing many professional players, particularly in Major League Baseball. Football (soccer) is also growing in popularity, especially after the national team's success in international tournaments.

- Education: Panama has a relatively high literacy rate, with education being compulsory for children between ages 6 and 15. There are public and private schools, and many students pursue higher education abroad, particularly in the United States.

- Hospitality: Panamanians are known for their warmth and friendliness. Visitors often find the people to be open and welcoming, reflecting the country's diverse and inclusive culture.

- Traditional Crafts: Handicrafts are an important part of Panama's cultural heritage. Traditional crafts include molas (textile art), woven baskets, wood carvings, and beaded jewelry, often made by Indigenous communities.

PANAMA'S POLITICAL HISTORY

- Colonial Era: Panama was part of the Spanish Empire from the early 16th century until the early 19th century. It was a key route for Spanish explorers and merchants due to its strategic location connecting the Pacific and Atlantic Oceans.

- The Role of Panama in the Spanish Empire: During the colonial period, Panama served as an important transit route for goods, gold, and silver between the Pacific and the Caribbean. The city of Panama City was founded in 1519 and became the first Spanish settlement on the Pacific coast.

- Independence from Spain: Panama gained independence from Spain on November 28, 1821, along with several other provinces in Central America. It initially became part of the United Provinces of the Americas, which later formed part of Gran Colombia under the leadership of Simón Bolívar.

- Part of Colombia: After Gran Colombia dissolved in 1831, Panama became a part of Colombia. This period was marked by tensions between Panama and the Colombian government, particularly over issues related to control of the Isthmus and the desire for greater autonomy.

- Separation from Colombia: In 1903, Panama declared its independence from Colombia, largely due to the longstanding tensions with the Colombian government and the desire to gain control over the construction of the Panama Canal. The separation was facilitated by the United States, which had significant interest in building the canal.

- The Panama Canal and U.S. Involvement: The United States played a key role in Panama's independence by providing military support in exchange for rights to build and control the Panama Canal. The Hay-Bunau-Varilla Treaty signed in 1903 granted the U.S. control over the Canal Zone.

- The Panama Canal: The Panama Canal, completed in 1914, is one of the most important waterways in the world, connecting the Atlantic and Pacific Oceans. It has been a significant factor in Panama's economy and international importance. The U.S. controlled the canal until 1999, when it was handed over to Panama under the Treaty of Torrijos-Carter (signed in 1977) and finalized in 1999.

- Military Dictatorship: From the 1960s to the 1980s, Panama was ruled by military regimes. The most notable figure during this period was Manuel Noriega, who became the de facto leader of the country in the 1980s. Noriega's regime was marked by corruption, human rights abuses, and involvement in drug trafficking.

- U.S. Invasion (1989): In December 1989, the United States invaded Panama in an operation known as Operation Just Cause. The invasion aimed to depose Manuel Noriega, restore democratic governance, safeguard U.S. citizens living in Panama, and address the growing influence of drug cartels. Noriega was captured, brought to the U.S., and tried for drug trafficking and other crimes.

- Return to Democracy: After the U.S. invasion, Panama transitioned back to civilian rule. In 1990, Guillermo Endara was elected as president, marking the return to democratic governance. The country has remained a democracy since then, with regular elections and peaceful transfers of power.

- Panama's Modern Political System: Panama is a democratic republic with a presidential system of government. The president is both the head of state and head of government. The country has a multi-party system, with elections held every five years.

- Political Parties: Panama's political landscape includes several major political parties, including the Democratic Revolutionary Party (PRD), the Panama Democratic Party (Panameñista), and the People's Party. Parties typically have diverse platforms, with varying stances on issues such as economic policy, social development, and relations with the U.S. and neighboring countries.

- The Panama Papers Scandal: In 2016, Panama was at the center of the Panama Papers scandal, which revealed how the country's law firms helped wealthy individuals and companies hide assets offshore. The scandal brought attention to Panama's role in global tax evasion and led to significant reforms in its financial sector.

- Panama's Foreign Relations: Panama maintains strong relationships with many countries, particularly the United States, due to the Panama Canal. It is a member of various international organizations, including the United Nations, World Bank, World Trade Organization (WTO), and Organization of American States (OAS).

- Panama's Role in Global Trade: With the Panama Canal as a major asset, Panama has become a global hub for trade and logistics. The country has established numerous free trade agreements, including with the U.S., Canada, and several Latin

American countries, and continues to grow as a key player in international commerce.

PANAMA CANAL: THE HEART OF THE NATION

- Historical Significance: The Panama Canal is one of the most significant engineering feats in history. It was completed in 1914 and serves as a crucial waterway connecting the Atlantic Ocean to the Pacific Ocean, drastically reducing the time needed for ships to travel between the two oceans.

- Construction and Development: The canal was initially conceived by the French engineer Ferdinand de Lesseps in the late 19th century but was abandoned due to engineering difficulties and disease (mainly malaria and yellow fever). The U.S. took over the project in 1904, under President Theodore Roosevelt, and completed it in 1914.

- Strategic Importance: The canal is of immense geopolitical and economic importance. It facilitates global trade by providing the shortest sea route between the Atlantic and Pacific Oceans, saving thousands of miles and weeks of travel for ships, especially in the transportation of goods like oil, minerals, and agricultural products.

PANAMA FACTS AND TRIVIA

- **Size and Dimensions**: The Panama Canal stretches about 50 miles (80 kilometers) across the Isthmus of Panama, connecting the Caribbean Sea to the Pacific Ocean. Ships navigate through the canal's system of locks, raising and lowering vessels over the 500-foot (150-meter) difference in elevation between the two oceans.

- **The Canal Locks**: The canal uses a system of three lock chambers (two on the Pacific side and one on the Atlantic side) to lift and lower ships. Each lock chamber is large enough to accommodate a full-sized ship, and each lock chamber uses approximately 26 million gallons (100 million liters) of water to raise and lower the vessels.

- **The Opening of the Canal**: The Panama Canal was officially opened on August 15, 1914, with the passage of the American ship SS Ancon, marking the completion of the project. The canal soon became a key route for international shipping.

- **The U.S. Control (1903-1999)**: From its completion in 1914 until 1999, the United States controlled the Panama Canal, as part of an agreement with Panama that had been formalized in the Hay-Bunau-Varilla Treaty (1903). The canal zone was under U.S. sovereignty until the Torrijos-Carter Treaties of 1977, which set the stage for Panama to regain control by December 31, 1999.

- **The Handing Over to Panama**: On December 31, 1999, the Panama Canal Authority (ACP), a Panamanian government entity, officially took control of the canal. This transition marked a pivotal moment in Panama's history, as it gained full sovereignty over one of the world's most important maritime trade routes.

- **Expansion and Modernization**: In 2016, the Panama Canal underwent a major expansion with the completion of the Third Set of Locks, also known as the Panama Canal Expansion Project. This project involved the construction of a new set of locks, allowing larger ships, known as Panamax or Post-Panamax vessels, to pass through the canal. The expansion has significantly increased the canal's capacity and its economic impact.

- Economic Impact: The Panama Canal is a primary driver of the country's economy, contributing to trade, shipping, and logistics. It generates significant revenue for Panama through tolls, with over 12,000 ships passing through it annually. The revenue helps fund the national economy and public services.

- Environmental Considerations: The canal has had significant environmental impacts on the region. Efforts have been made to balance its operational needs with the conservation of local ecosystems. The Panama Canal Authority works to maintain the surrounding rainforests, as the canal is surrounded by the Soberanía National Park, a critical area for biodiversity.

- The Canal's Cultural Impact: The Panama Canal is a symbol of Panama's national identity and pride. It is a major tourist attraction, with visitors coming to see the locks in operation, visit the Panama Canal Museum in Panama City, and explore the canal's surrounding areas.

- Security: The canal is a critical part of global trade, and as such, its security is of national and international concern. Panama works closely with global security organizations to safeguard the canal from potential threats, including natural disasters, military conflicts, and environmental risks.

- Panama Canal Authority (ACP): The ACP is the governmental entity responsible for operating, maintaining, and expanding the canal. It oversees the logistics, revenue generation, and operational management of the waterway, ensuring it remains a vital asset for global trade.

- Future Developments: Panama continues to invest in modernizing the canal and surrounding infrastructure to meet the demands of global trade. This includes expanding port facilities, improving logistics networks, and addressing environmental concerns to ensure the canal remains efficient and sustainable for years to come.

ECONOMY AND INDUSTRY

- Overview of Panama's Economy: Panama has one of the most stable and prosperous economies in Latin America. The country's economy is service-based, with a focus on banking, trade, logistics, and tourism. It has enjoyed steady growth, driven in large part by the Panama Canal and its strategic location.

- The Panama Canal's Economic Importance: The Panama Canal is the cornerstone of Panama's economy. It generates significant revenue through tolls, which contribute to public finances and economic growth. The canal also drives trade-related industries, such as logistics, shipping, and port operations.

- Trade and Commerce: Panama is one of the most important trade hubs in the world. It is strategically located at the crossroads of the Americas, serving as a key transshipment point for goods moving between North America, South America, Europe, and Asia. The country has extensive trade relationships, especially with the United States, China, and other countries in the region.

- **Banking and Finance**: Panama is a major financial center in Latin America. Its banking sector is highly developed, with numerous international banks and financial institutions based in Panama City. The country has favorable tax laws, banking secrecy, and a robust regulatory framework, making it a popular destination for international investors and corporations.

- **U.S. Dollar Economy**: Panama uses the U.S. dollar (USD) alongside its own currency, the balboa (PAB), which is pegged at par to the dollar. This dollarized economy helps to maintain stability, attract foreign investment, and facilitate international trade.

- **Free Trade Zones and Colon Free Trade Zone**: Panama has established several free trade zones, the most prominent being the Colon Free Trade Zone (CFTZ), located near the Caribbean coast. The CFTZ is the largest free trade zone in the Americas, providing tax exemptions and other incentives for businesses engaged in import/export and re-export activities.

- **Tourism Industry**: Tourism is a significant part of Panama's economy. The country offers a wide variety of attractions, from the Panama Canal and historical sites to beautiful beaches, rainforests, and diverse wildlife. Major tourist destinations include Panama City, the San Blas Islands, Bocas del Toro, and Boquete.

- **Agriculture**: Agriculture plays a smaller but still important role in Panama's economy. Key agricultural exports include bananas, pineapples, coffee, sugar, and cocoa. The country also produces vegetables, such as tomatoes, onions, and potatoes, primarily for local consumption.

- **Fishing and Seafood**: Panama has a thriving fishing industry, particularly in seafood exports. The country is one of the top exporters of tuna and shrimp, which are important products for both local consumption and international markets.

- Mining Industry: Panama has some mineral resources, and mining is a growing industry. The country is home to the Cobre Panamá mine, one of the largest copper mines in the world. Copper is the primary mineral extracted, but the country also has gold, silver, and other mineral deposits.

- Construction and Infrastructure: Panama has experienced rapid growth in the construction and infrastructure sectors, especially in Panama City, where the skyline is dotted with modern skyscrapers and luxury developments. The government has invested heavily in improving transportation infrastructure, including roads, bridges, and public transportation.

- Energy Sector: The energy sector in Panama is mainly based on hydropower, with a large portion of the country's electricity generated through hydroelectric plants. Panama also imports petroleum for industrial and transportation use. The government has been making efforts to diversify energy sources, including exploring solar power and wind energy.

- Industrialization and Manufacturing: Panama's industrial sector is relatively small, but it includes the manufacturing of products such as textiles, food and beverages, pharmaceuticals, and electrical machinery. The Colon Free Zone has been a key driver for manufacturing and assembly operations for export.

- Foreign Direct Investment (FDI): Panama attracts significant foreign direct investment, primarily due to its strategic location, business-friendly environment, and favorable tax policies. Major sectors attracting FDI include real estate, banking, tourism, infrastructure, and transportation.

- Labor Force: Panama has a relatively young labor force, with many people employed in the service sector, including banking, tourism, and trade. The country has a relatively high literacy rate and a growing middle class. However, there are challenges related to income inequality and unemployment in rural areas.

- **Poverty and Income Inequality**: While Panama has one of the highest per capita incomes in Latin America, there is significant income inequality, especially between urban and rural areas. Poverty rates are higher in rural and Indigenous communities, though the country has made strides in improving social services and poverty alleviation programs.

- **Panama's Role in Global Trade**: As a global shipping hub, Panama plays an essential role in facilitating international trade. It is part of several trade agreements, including the **Central America Free Trade Agreement (CAFTA)** and the **Free Trade Agreement (FTA)** with the United States, and it continues to expand its trade relationships with countries like China.

- **Challenges and Future Prospects**: Panama faces several economic challenges, including reducing poverty, improving education and healthcare, and addressing environmental concerns related to deforestation and climate change. However, its strategic location, canal revenue, and growing sectors such as tourism and services position it well for continued economic growth.

PANAMA'S CUISINE

- Diverse Influences: Panamanian cuisine is a rich fusion of flavors influenced by Indigenous, African, Spanish, and Afro-Caribbean cultures. The country's geographic location and historical trade routes have also played a role in shaping the variety of ingredients and cooking styles.

- Staple Foods: Rice is a staple in Panama, often served with beans, plantains, and meat. Corn is also a key ingredient, used in dishes like arepas (cornmeal cakes) and empanadas (fried turnovers).

- Sancocho: Sancocho is a traditional Panamanian dish, a chicken soup made with yuca (cassava root), corn on the cob, potatoes, and herbs. It is often enjoyed during celebrations or as a remedy for colds.

- Arroz con Pollo: Arroz con pollo (rice with chicken) is a beloved and common dish throughout Panama. The rice is often cooked with vegetables and spices, and the chicken is usually stewed in the same pot, creating a flavorful, comforting meal.

- **Tamales**: Tamales are a popular dish in Panama, especially during the holiday season. They are made by wrapping corn dough around a filling of meat, chicken, or vegetables, and then steaming them in plantain leaves. This dish is similar to others found throughout Latin America.

- **Ceviche**: Panama's coastal location makes ceviche a popular dish. Made from fresh, raw fish or shrimp, ceviche is marinated in lime juice with onions, peppers, cilantro, and other seasonings. It's often served as a refreshing appetizer.

- **Ropa Vieja**: Ropa vieja, which translates to "old clothes," is a dish of shredded beef cooked in a tomato-based sauce with peppers, onions, garlic, and spices. It is commonly served with rice and beans, offering a flavorful and filling meal.

- **Yuca**: Yuca, also known as cassava, is a root vegetable widely used in Panamanian cooking. It can be boiled, fried, or mashed, and is often served as a side dish with meats or fish.

- **Panamanian Stew**: Panamanian stews, such as carne guisada (beef stew), are commonly served with rice. The beef is slowly cooked in a rich, flavorful sauce made from tomatoes, onions, and spices, and the dish is often accompanied by fried plantains or corn tortillas.

- **Patacones**: Patacones are fried green plantains that are smashed and then fried again until crispy. These are commonly served as a side dish or snack and can be dipped in sauces such as salsa rosada (a mix of ketchup and mayonnaise).

- **Coconut Rice (Arroz con Coco)**: A popular dish on the Caribbean coast of Panama is arroz con coco (coconut rice). The rice is cooked with coconut milk, giving it a rich, creamy flavor, and it is often served alongside fish or other seafood.

- **Chicheme**: Chicheme is a traditional Panamanian drink made from corn, milk, sugar, and spices. It is a sweet and creamy beverage that is often consumed as a refreshing treat, particularly in rural areas.

- **Pipian**: Pipian is a rich sauce made from pumpkin, peanuts, and spices. It is often used to accompany meat dishes, such as chicken or pork, and adds a creamy, nutty flavor to the meal.

- **Fried Fish**: Being a coastal country, Panama has a strong seafood culture. Fried fish, such as red snapper or tilapia, is often served with rice, salad, and fried plantains.

- **Arepas**: While originally from Venezuela and Colombia, arepas are also popular in Panama. These cornmeal cakes are often filled with cheese, meat, or eggs, and they can be served as a snack or breakfast item.

- **Desserts**: Traditional desserts in Panama include dulce de leche (a caramelized milk-based sweet), tres leches cake (a sponge cake soaked in three types of milk), and coconut-based sweets. These desserts often feature the sweet and rich flavors of local ingredients like coconut and sugar cane.

- **Panamanian Coffee**: Panama is known for its coffee, particularly the high-quality Boquete coffee, grown in the cool mountain region of the same name. The coffee is known for its smooth, mild flavor, and it is a point of pride for Panamanians.

- **Festive Foods**: During Panama's Carnival season, traditional foods like empanadas, tamales, and sweet treats are commonly enjoyed. These foods reflect the festive and communal nature of the celebration.

- **Fried Pork**: Fried pork (called lechón in some areas) is a beloved dish, especially during major holidays. The pork is seasoned with spices and slow-cooked until it becomes tender, and then deep-fried for a crispy exterior.

- **Seafood and Shellfish**: Due to Panama's proximity to both the Pacific and Caribbean Oceans, the country offers a wide variety of seafood. Crab, lobster, octopus, and mussels are commonly prepared in stews, grilled, or fried.

TOURISM AND TRAVEL IN PANAMA

- Tourism's Economic Importance: Tourism is a vital part of Panama's economy. The country attracts visitors from around the world due to its rich history, diverse culture, natural beauty, and the world-famous Panama Canal. In recent years, tourism has grown steadily, contributing significantly to the nation's GDP.

- Panama City: Panama City is a major urban center and a key tourist destination. The city is known for its modern skyline, historic Old Town (Casco Viejo), and proximity to the Panama Canal. Visitors can explore landmarks like the Panama Canal Museum, Metropolitan Natural Park, and the Biodiversity Museum designed by architect Frank Gehry.

- Panama Canal: The Panama Canal is one of the most iconic attractions in the country. Visitors can tour the Miraflores Locks Visitor Center, where they can watch ships passing through the canal, learn about its history, and explore interactive exhibits. The canal is not only a marvel of engineering but also a symbol of Panama's global importance.

PANAMA FACTS AND TRIVIA

- Bocas del Toro: Located on the Caribbean coast, Bocas del Toro is a popular travel destination known for its idyllic beaches, crystal-clear waters, and vibrant marine life. The archipelago consists of several islands, including Isla Colón, the main island, and offers activities like snorkeling, scuba diving, and surfing.

- San Blas Islands: The San Blas Islands (Guna Yala) are a group of more than 360 islands, famous for their pristine beaches, turquoise waters, and the rich culture of the Guna people. The islands are an off-the-beaten-path destination offering unique cultural experiences and natural beauty.

- Boquete: Situated in the highlands of western Panama, Boquete is a charming town known for its cool climate, coffee plantations, and outdoor activities. Visitors come to hike the famous Volcán Barú, Panama's highest peak, or to tour the coffee farms that produce some of the world's finest coffee, particularly Boquete coffee.

- Darien National Park: Darien National Park is a UNESCO World Heritage site and one of Panama's most biodiverse areas. It is located in the Darien province along the border with Colombia. The park is home to numerous species of wildlife, including jaguars, monkeys, and rare birds, and offers opportunities for ecotourism and adventure travel.

- Panama's Beaches: Panama boasts over 2,400 kilometers (1,500 miles) of coastline along both the Pacific and Caribbean Oceans, making it a prime destination for beach lovers. Popular beach destinations include Santa Catalina, known for surfing, Las Lajas, and Playa Venao, ideal for relaxation and water sports.

- Azuero Peninsula: The Azuero Peninsula is an area rich in cultural heritage, with small towns like Pedasí known for their traditional festivals, festivals, and agriculture. Visitors can explore the Cerro Hoya National Park or attend events such as the

Carnival de Las Tablas, one of Panama's largest and most vibrant carnivals.

• Gatun Lake and Panama Canal Railway: Gatun Lake, formed by the construction of the Panama Canal, is a popular spot for eco-tours. Visitors can take boat tours to spot wildlife, including crocodiles and monkeys. Another popular way to experience the canal is by riding the historic Panama Canal Railway, which runs from Panama City to Colón, offering beautiful views of the canal and surrounding rainforest.

• Volcan Baru: Volcán Barú is the highest point in Panama, located in Chiriquí Province. It is a popular destination for hiking, offering spectacular panoramic views of both the Pacific Ocean and Caribbean Sea on clear days. The summit is also known for its diverse flora and fauna.

• Rainforests and Eco-Tourism: Panama is home to rich and diverse rainforests, offering opportunities for eco-tourism. The Soberanía National Park and La Amistad International Park are two of the most famous, where visitors can go bird-watching, hike through dense jungle, and spot wildlife like sloths, toucans, and frogs.

• Cultural Tourism: Panama is known for its vibrant culture, which blends Indigenous, Afro-Caribbean, and European traditions. Tourists can experience this mix through music, dance, festivals, and cuisine. Panama City hosts several cultural events, such as the Panama Jazz Festival, and visitors can also explore traditional Indigenous villages.

• Shopping: Panama offers great shopping opportunities, particularly in Panama City, with its modern malls, local markets, and tax-free shopping areas. Albrook Mall is one of the largest shopping centers in Latin America, and Panama's Duty-Free Zones offer visitors the chance to buy luxury goods at discounted prices.

PANAMA FACTS AND TRIVIA

- Adventure Travel: Panama is a destination for adventure seekers, with activities such as white-water rafting in the Chiriquí River, hiking in cloud forests, zip-lining in rainforests, surfing on both the Pacific and Caribbean coasts, and kayaking through mangroves.

- Panama's Festivals: Panama is known for its lively festivals, which reflect the nation's rich cultural traditions. Key festivals include Carnival, celebrated with parades, costumes, and music, the Panama Jazz Festival, and Fiestas Patrias (Patriotic Holidays), where the country's independence from Spain and Colombia is commemorated.

- Health and Wellness Tourism: Panama has emerged as a destination for health and wellness tourism. The country offers wellness resorts and spas located in serene natural settings, where visitors can enjoy yoga retreats, detox programs, and medical tourism services, such as dental care and cosmetic surgery, at competitive prices.

- Transport and Accessibility: Panama's central location in the Americas makes it an accessible destination. The country's Tocumen International Airport in Panama City is one of the busiest in Latin America, with direct flights to major cities around the world. Panama's public transportation system includes buses, metro, taxis, and domestic flights, making it easy for visitors to travel around the country.

- Safety for Tourists: Panama is generally considered a safe destination for tourists. While it is always advisable to take standard precautions, particularly in crowded areas, Panama has a relatively low crime rate compared to other Central American countries. It is a popular destination for solo travelers, families, and adventure seekers alike.

- Sustainability and Eco-Friendly Travel: Panama is increasingly focusing on sustainable tourism practices. Many eco-lodges, national parks, and nature reserves in the country are committed to preserving the environment and promoting responsible tourism, offering eco-conscious travelers a chance to experience Panama's natural wonders while minimizing their ecological footprint.

WILDLIFE AND BIODIVERSITY

- Biodiversity Hotspot: Panama is one of the most biodiverse countries in the world. Despite its small size, it is home to thousands of species of plants, animals, and insects. The country's unique location between the Pacific Ocean and the Caribbean Sea makes it a natural bridge for species migration and contributes to its rich biodiversity.

- Tropical Rainforests: Panama's tropical rainforests, particularly in regions like the Darien and Bocas del Toro, are some of the most biologically diverse ecosystems in the world. These forests are teeming with diverse species of plants, animals, and insects, many of which are endemic to the region.

- Panama's Flora: Panama has a wide range of plant species, with an estimated 10,000 species of plants, including orchids, palms, and ferns. Notably, Panama is home to the Gatun Lake area, which has a variety of tropical plants and is an essential ecological zone for conservation efforts.

- Endangered Species: Panama is home to several endangered species, many of which are found only in this region. These include the Panamanian golden frog (Atelopus zeteki), an iconic amphibian, and the harpy eagle, the largest eagle species in the world, which resides in the tropical rainforests.

• Panama Canal's Role in Biodiversity: The Panama Canal serves as a critical migration route for species moving between the Pacific and Atlantic Oceans. As a result, the canal watershed is an important area for biodiversity conservation. Many species that live along the canal and its surrounding ecosystems are protected by Panama's environmental laws.

• Wildlife Corridors: Panama is creating protected wildlife corridors to help preserve the movement of species across various ecosystems. These corridors are vital for maintaining genetic diversity and reducing human-wildlife conflict, particularly as forests are cleared for development.

• Monkeys: Panama is home to several species of monkeys, including the Howler monkey, White-faced capuchin, and Spider monkey. These species are commonly seen in the forests and national parks, and their vocalizations are a characteristic feature of the Panamanian jungle.

• Birdwatching: Panama is a birdwatcher's paradise. Over 970 species of birds have been recorded in the country, including the Resplendent quetzal, Scarlet macaw, Harpy eagle, and Brown pelican. The Soberanía National Park near Panama City is one of the best places for birdwatching.

• Jaguar and Big Cats: The elusive jaguar, which is the largest cat in the Americas, roams Panama's forests. Other big cats found in Panama include the puma and ocelot. These animals are crucial to the balance of the ecosystems they inhabit.

• Reptiles and Amphibians: Panama is home to many species of reptiles, including turtles, iguanas, and crocodiles. The country is particularly known for its colorful amphibians, like the

Golden Poison Dart Frog and the Panamanian golden frog, which are vital to the local ecosystem.

- Marine Life: Panama's coasts, both in the Pacific and Caribbean, are rich in marine biodiversity. Coral reefs, including those near Coiba Island (a UNESCO World Heritage Site), are home to a variety of marine species such as sea turtles, sharks, rays, and countless species of fish. The waters also host important migratory species like whale sharks and humpback whales.

- Biodiversity Conservation: Panama has a robust system of protected areas, including national parks and wildlife reserves. These protected areas cover around 30% of the country's land area. Notable conservation areas include Coiba National Park, Darien National Park, and Volcán Barú National Park.

- Coiba Island: Coiba Island is a biodiversity hotspot and a UNESCO World Heritage Site, renowned for its unique marine and terrestrial species. It is home to a variety of endemic species, such as the Coiba island howler monkey, and its surrounding waters are a sanctuary for marine life like whales, dolphins, and sea turtles.

- Insects and Pollinators: Panama is home to a wide variety of insects, including many species of butterflies, beetles, and moths. The Panama Canal is also important for pollinators, such as bees, which help maintain agricultural productivity in the region.

- The Darien Gap: The Darien Gap is a vast, undeveloped area of rainforest that stretches along the border with Colombia. This area is a critical habitat for a wide range of wildlife, including the Jaguar, Tapir, and Harpy eagle. The Darien region is remote, with only a few roads, and remains largely pristine.

- Marine Turtles: Panama's beaches are important nesting grounds for several species of marine turtles, including the Leatherback, Green, and Olive Ridley turtles. Conservation efforts are in place to protect nesting sites along the Pacific and Caribbean coasts, where turtle populations are monitored and protected from poaching.

- Ecotourism: Panama has embraced ecotourism, offering visitors the chance to experience the country's incredible biodiversity in a sustainable way. Popular ecotourism activities include guided wildlife tours, birdwatching, trekking through rainforests, and visits to national parks and reserves.

- Endemic Species: Panama is home to many endemic species—species found nowhere else in the world. These include unique frogs like the Panamanian golden frog, various species of birds, and specialized plants that thrive only in Panama's unique ecosystems.

- Mangroves: Panama's coastal areas, especially in the Bocas del Toro and Guna Yala regions, feature extensive mangrove forests. These ecosystems provide critical breeding grounds for fish and other marine life, and they serve as natural barriers protecting coastal areas from erosion and storms.

- Conservation Challenges: Despite its wealth of biodiversity, Panama faces conservation challenges such as deforestation, illegal wildlife trade, and the impacts of climate change. The government and non-governmental organizations are working to address these issues through conservation programs, wildlife protection laws, and habitat restoration efforts.

PANAMA TODAY AND TOMORROW

- Economic Growth: Panama has experienced consistent economic growth over the past few decades. The country has become one of the fastest-growing economies in Latin America, largely driven by the Panama Canal, banking sector, trade, and increasing tourism. The country is often seen as a stable and prosperous example in the region.

- Global Trade Hub: Panama continues to be a key player in global trade, thanks to the Panama Canal and its strategic location. The expansion of the canal, completed in 2016, has further boosted Panama's significance in international shipping. The country serves as a transit hub for goods moving between the Atlantic and Pacific Oceans.

- Infrastructure Development: The government of Panama is focused on infrastructure development, particularly in transportation, energy, and public services. Major projects include the expansion of Panama City's Metro, new roads, and the development of airport facilities, which help strengthen the country's position as a regional transportation hub.

- Panama Canal Expansion: The Panama Canal Expansion, which added new larger locks and channels, allows the passage of Post-Panamax ships, which are too large to fit through the original locks. This expansion has significantly increased traffic through the canal and contributed to Panama's growing influence in global trade.

- Sustainable Development: Panama is making efforts to balance economic growth with environmental sustainability. The country is investing in renewable energy sources such as hydropower, solar, and wind energy, while also focusing on the protection of natural resources and biodiversity. Panama has committed to reducing carbon emissions and increasing its environmental awareness.

- Tourism Growth: Panama's tourism sector has been expanding rapidly. With a variety of natural, cultural, and historical attractions, the country continues to attract visitors from all over the world. Key initiatives are underway to promote ecotourism, adventure tourism, and cultural heritage tourism, which allow visitors to experience Panama's diverse offerings in a sustainable manner.

- Digital Transformation: Panama is focusing on digital innovation and the development of a knowledge-based economy. With investments in technology, financial services, and startups, Panama is positioning itself as a regional tech hub. The country is also embracing the digital economy, with growth in e-commerce, fintech, and IT services.

- Panama as a Financial Center: Panama is known as a major financial center in Latin America. The country's banking and finance sector continues to grow, with Panama City housing a significant number of international banks and financial institutions. The country offers tax incentives for businesses and is a popular destination for foreign investment.

• Social Challenges: Despite its economic growth, Panama faces several social challenges, including poverty, income inequality, and education gaps. The government is working to address these issues by improving public services, increasing access to education, and focusing on social welfare programs, particularly in rural and indigenous communities.

• Urbanization and Infrastructure: Panama City, the capital, has seen rapid urbanization, with a growing skyline and improved infrastructure. The city is becoming more cosmopolitan, attracting both expatriates and businesses. However, urban growth is putting pressure on housing, traffic congestion, and public services, which the government is working to address with ongoing urban planning initiatives.

• Indigenous Rights and Inclusion: Panama has a significant Indigenous population, and their rights and inclusion in society remain a key issue. Indigenous communities, such as the Guna, Ngäbe-Buglé, and Emberá, are working toward greater autonomy, land rights, and access to services. The country is moving toward greater recognition of cultural diversity and the rights of indigenous peoples.

• Youth Empowerment: Panama's youth population is growing, and there is a strong emphasis on improving access to education and employment opportunities for young people. With a relatively young workforce, Panama is focusing on fostering talent in fields like technology, engineering, and business to ensure a sustainable future workforce.

• Health and Well-Being: Panama's healthcare system is improving, with efforts to expand access to quality care across both urban and rural areas. The government is working to address challenges in public health infrastructure, and Panama is known for its medical tourism industry, attracting visitors seeking affordable medical treatments, including dental and cosmetic surgeries.

• Environmental Preservation: As a country with a wealth of natural beauty and biodiversity, Panama is committed to environmental preservation. Protected areas, such as national parks and wildlife reserves, continue to be a priority, with a focus on sustainable development. Panama is also making strides in tackling issues like deforestation and water conservation.

• Regional Leadership: Panama plays an active role in Central America's political and economic affairs. As a member of the Central American Integration System (SICA), Panama is working to enhance cooperation on regional issues such as trade, security, and environmental sustainability.

• Cultural Renaissance: Panama is undergoing a cultural renaissance, with the promotion of its rich cultural heritage, including music, dance, and art. Festivals like Carnival, the Panama Jazz Festival, and the International Film Festival highlight Panama's growing cultural scene, which is increasingly being recognized on the global stage.

• International Relations: Panama has strong international relations with countries across the globe, with active participation in organizations like the United Nations, World Trade Organization (WTO), and Organization of American States (OAS). The country's diplomatic efforts focus on global cooperation on issues like climate change, trade, and peacekeeping.

• Smart Cities and Innovation: Panama is looking to develop smart cities that incorporate technology, sustainability, and efficient infrastructure. The government is also working on public-private partnerships to modernize urban areas and make them more livable, efficient, and environmentally friendly.

- **The Future of the Panama Canal**: The Panama Canal continues to be a critical asset for the country. The government is focusing on its future by investing in maintenance and modernization, ensuring that the canal remains a hub for global shipping and trade for decades to come.

- **Challenges of Climate Change**: Panama faces threats from climate change, including rising sea levels, extreme weather events, and changes in rainfall patterns. The country is investing in strategies for disaster resilience, sustainable land use, and improving its infrastructure to adapt to the changing climate.

www.ingramcontent.com/pod-product-compliance
Lightning Source LLC
LaVergne TN
LVHW020523130225
803513LV00008B/194